Winning the War for Profit
Developing Leaders
Where It Really Matters

Penny D. Miller, SPHR, SHRM-SCP

ACKNOWLEDGEMENTS

Many thanks to those in the SPS Mastermind Community who gave their opinions, encouragement and support from idea to book launch.

Thanks, Don Swift, Don Swift and Associates, for reading the draft and providing your expertise.

DEDICATION

To those Noncommissioned Officers who gave me their knowledge, support, and advice through 21 years of service, and who continue to groom the young men and women of the military today.

TABLE OF CONTENTS

Introduction

"Today, no leader can afford to be indifferent to the challenge of engaging employees in the work of creating the future. Engagement may have been optional in the past, but it's pretty much the whole game today."
– Gary Hamel

The marketplace is competitive, and much of an organization's success hinges upon its people. But by nearly every measure, organizations are not doing a good job of getting the most from this vital resource. This is especially true at the first-line supervisor level.

Approximately 40% of newly-promoted managers are no longer in their jobs 18 months later. Either they have been fired, have quit, or have returned to their previous positions. This churn is not good for the organization or for your employees.

As an example, I conduct a four-month leadership development program. Many of the participants are first-line supervisors, because that is where I think companies get the best return on their investment.

At one company, one of the classes consisted almost entirely of people who had been promoted into a first-line supervisory position and failed, returning to their previous jobs. The company was getting ready to promote them all back into supervisory positions, but decided to invest in a little training first.

All of the participants told me they wished they had the training before they were promoted the first time. It would have saved them and the company a lot of stress. At the same time, I have to congratulate the company leadership for recognizing a problem and taking action to correct it.

We can do better, and in this book, I'm going to show you how. If you want to have a more effective, more profitable business, this book is for you. I tend to be a bottom-line person. You won't find a lot of fluff in this book. Instead, this book is a step-by-step guide to strengthening your team at the all-important supervisor level.

I have been working with managers at all levels for over 30 years. In recent years, I have focused on training and coaching managers, especially first-line supervisors, to make them more effective. I have gleaned pointers from hundreds of books and audios, but more importantly, have watched and learned about selecting, development, and support of supervisors from some of the best (and worst) organizations.

One of the best is the U.S. Armed Forces. You'll see I have adopted a life-cycle approach as it is used by the military, even though we're only looking at the first-line supervisor level in this book.

By following the process outlined in this book, you'll have more successful supervisors, happier employees, and a more profitable company.

Does this sound like I am over-promising? I'm not.

The military has studied leadership for thousands of years. Those leaders have induced people to follow them under some austere and stressful conditions. In the modern era, people have responded, not because of fear, but because of the desire to follow. The techniques are directly transferable to the business world.

If you will take the steps presented here and follow through, your organization will be more cohesive, more effective, and more profitable.

Let's get started.

Foreword

"If you don't have a competitive advantage, don't compete."
— Jack Welch

My very first job (other than babysitting) was as a supervisor. I had never worked in any organization, and really had little clue what I was getting into. But I went from a full-time college student to a commissioned officer in the United States Air Force, responsible for running a work center at 22 years of age.

Fortunately for me, I was in the military. If there is any organization in the United States that has paid attention to developing leaders, it is the military. I am thankful that that is where I learned to lead. Even more importantly from my perspective, the military understands that leadership at that very first rung of the management ladder is critical to operational success and doesn't stint on preparing and training the people they assign to these vital jobs.

I was assigned an NCO who was responsible for training me. I didn't know much about the military and less about leading people, but I was smart enough to know I didn't know anything. I was fortunate to serve with some great non-commissioned officers who did their best to train up "the butterbar" in a way that has served me well in the years since, and to start my career with a few officer mentors that did their best to teach me the ropes.

You'll see the influence of the military in the approach I take to developing supervisors.

Most civilian organizations throw their new supervisors into the deep end of the pool. If the new supervisor manages to dog paddle fast enough, long enough, he'll survive.

If he doesn't, the organization will pick the next person and toss her in—and they'll continue that process until they get at least satisfactory success.

It's a brutal, haphazard, and ineffective approach to choosing, training, and supporting people who really are the key to organizational success. If you want to have a high-performance organization, you can't afford to overlook your supervisors.

Overall, the process is relatively straightforward. That doesn't mean it's easy or foolproof, but we can greatly improve our success with just a few processes, providing we are conscientious about implementing them and tenacious about seeing them through.

That's why I wrote this little book. I hope organizations will harvest the benefits of having the right people with the right skills in these critical positions, and that fewer supervisors will fail in their new roles.

Chapter 1

Why Supervisors Are So Important

"America's competitive advantage lies in its human talent. All of us should be doing everything we can to cultivate and develop our workforce."
— Elaine Chao

If you are in business, your goal is to make money. Preferably, more money than you're spending. In the best of all worlds, you'll make enough money to give yourself and your employees a decent paycheck and to reinvest in your business.

That being the case, I would argue there is no better place to invest dollars than in your first-line supervisors.

Not every business owner gets this. At one of my previous places of employment, the owners decided they needed to save on payroll. We had a very flat organizational structure.

One of the owners asked me, "Why don't we get rid of all of the supervisors? They get paid a lot and they don't really do anything."

At that time, we had around 350 employees, eight first-line supervisors, three senior managers, and 53 owners. Knowing the owner as I did, I just said, "So, you're okay talking to your receptionist yourself if you are unhappy with her performance?"

To which the reply was, "No, I don't want to deal with that."

Jobs saved.

But first-line supervisors are important for so much more than just keeping those higher up the chain from having to deal with unpleasant conversations with employees.

Most leadership studies and leadership trainings focus on the people at the top of the organizational ladder. Those people are important, but any of us who have been anywhere near the top know that it doesn't matter what grand vision we have, if the people in the organization do not support you in the day-to-day actions necessary to convert your vision into reality, it will never happen.

Organizations that truly want to thrive need to focus on that very first step of the leadership ladder. Unfortunately, that bottom rung is the leadership rung most ignored.

When I first started looking at background material for this book, I looked for academic research specifically about what it takes to succeed as a front-line supervisor, and was surprised to find there isn't much.

I even sent a research request to the Society for Human Resource Management Knowledge Center. What I got back was a long bibliography of articles about supervisor errors that landed the employer in hot water and cost them big dollars in fines and lawyer fees.

That seems to be the primary focus of supervisor training—risk management. The focus is on how not to make the big mistakes that will lead to legal hot water, instead of how to actually grow and develop people to allow the company to compete successfully in the marketplace. That's unfortunate, because that is really where the money is made.

I am happy to say that in the last year or two, I have seen a few studies oriented toward discovering how important supervisors are and the necessity of preparing and supporting them in their roles.

We'll talk about a couple of those, but first, I want to give you two anecdotal stories to illustrate how I know—even without hard, empirical evidence— how critical supervisors are.

Saving Airman "Smith"

In the first case, I had a young man show up in my unit overseas. Practically as soon as he landed, he was selected for a random urinalysis. He was positive for marijuana.

At that time, it was possible for a young airman to remain in the military with one positive urinalysis, although there would be some punishment.

Unfortunately for this young man, he came up for another random test before we got the results of the first test back. Since these tests took place so close to one another, it too came back positive for marijuana. The Air Force may have accepted one positive test, but two? Things were looking bleak for my airman.

The airman was about 21 and had a wife and baby. I asked him if he was willing to do whatever was necessary to stay in the Air Force or would he prefer to hang it up and go home. His response was that he would do what was necessary. I decided to take a risk.

I had originally intended to assign the airman to the section of my greatest organizational need. However, in light of the circumstances, I decided a different approach was in order.

I decided to assign him instead to my best NCO. I knew that supervisor would hold the airman to high standards. The airman would excel or he would go home.

I didn't want to take a chance that another supervisor might allow the airman to coast by, which would perhaps encourage him to be lackadaisical toward his work, and encourage him to conclude we would be lax in enforcement of drug standards.

My strategy worked, in part because the airman made a commitment to change, and in part because his supervisor led by example, set a high standard, and ensured this airman (and the other airmen assigned to him) met that standard.

Not only did the airman meet standards, he later was recognized as Airman of the Quarter and was eventually promoted below the zone to senior airman (an accelerated promotion in recognition of outstanding performance.)

I attribute much of Airman Smith's success (as did he) to having a supervisor that demanded excellent performance, modeled the right behaviors, and coached/mentored the people who worked for him. Airman Smith might have been able to stay out of trouble with any good supervisor, but a top-shelf supervisor helped him elevate his performance from satisfactory to outstanding.

As a result of this match, my airman made the necessary behavior change, resulting in less turnover for my department, a dedicated employee, and higher performance.

A Tale of Two Supervisors

Later in my career, I had a work center that was floundering badly. Internal audits showed that the work coming from that work center was neither accurate nor timely.

The individuals in that work center were working hard, to include a lot of overtime, but they weren't making progress. The employees were frustrated, even though they liked their supervisor. They were tired of the overtime, the customer complaints, and their coworkers in other departments belittling them because of their poor-quality work.

The supervisor argued that the problems were caused by a lack of manpower. I gave him additional staffing, but the situation didn't improve.

I decided to change the supervisor. It wasn't a popular decision—as I said, the employees in that work center liked the supervisor, as he had a friendly, outgoing personality.

The supervisor I moved into the section ran a tight ship. Again, he set high performance standards and enforced them. Just as importantly, he invested a lot of time in training his employees (the previous supervisor "didn't have time" to train his people.)

Within 90 days, the audit rosters were cleaned up, the backlog of work was gone, the extra staffing was released back to other requirements, and there was no more overtime.

The employees didn't like the new supervisor initially (in fact, "didn't like" is probably a little mild for their feelings) but they respected him a lot by the end of the first month and wanted to keep him by the end of the 90 days.

Regardless of the scientific findings, these two stories and dozens more like them illustrate why the supervisor is so important. But let's review some of the recent findings anyway.

I am going to focus for a moment on a report from Harvard Business Review called *Frontline Managers: Are They Given the Leadership Tools to Succeed?* In a survey, senior management said that frontline managers are important to achieving business priorities.

Between 70% and 80% agreed that frontline managers were very important in:

- Achieving a high level of customer service
- Helping the organization achieve business goals
- Achieving high productivity
- Achieving high employee engagement
- Contributing to effective communication

But when asked how proficient their supervisors were at various skills they considered important, they agreed the answer was "not so much." Citing only two specific competencies, only 33% felt their frontline managers were proficient at business-based decision-making.

Only 20% were proficient at developing talent.

Ninety-two percent of these same senior managers believed frontline managers' lack of leadership development negatively impacted employee engagement and 79% believed the lack of leadership development moderately or negatively impacted the organization's performance.

Given all of this, these same leaders invest heavily in choosing and developing these frontline leaders, right? This is where the behavior and logic break down. It makes you wonder about the business-based decision making of our senior managers. Only 19% of companies felt their supervisor training was average to excellent and only 12% felt they invested enough in training. Why is that?

We say that supervisors are very important at mission-critical functions. We admit that our supervisors lack the skills to be successful in those tasks. But we admit we are not investing enough in training. You have to ask the question, "Why?" There are two main reasons.

First, companies frequently skimp on development dollars because of focus on profitability. Training dollars are some of the first dollars cut when financial resources are tight. Training is considered a "nice to have" instead of a "necessary to have." This behavior occurs in opposition to studies that have shown that companies that maintain their training in the face of recession do better during the recession and come out of the economic downturn in great position to capitalize on the economic recovery. Our focus on short-term earnings negatively impacts our long-term success.

Secondly, companies rely upon the trickle-down model for leadership development. In other words, higher level managers get development first, with the expectation that knowledge will "trickle down" to lower level managers. This theory of leadership development works about as well as the trickle down economic theory.

Here are just a few other reasons to focus on your supervisors:

- The right managers contribute <u>48% more profit</u> than average managers. (Frontline Managers, 2014)
- Managers account for at least 70% of the variance in employee engagement scores across business units. (Beck, 2014)
- Businesses say that manager and supervisor involvement was "extremely important" or "very important" to the success of their change efforts. (*Manager/Supervisor's Role in Change Management,* 2016)
- Total return to shareholders (TRS) over a 3-year period is 286% higher for those companies with a high level of employee trust versus those with a low level of trust, according to Watson Wyatt.
- Ninety-one percent of employees rated their relationship with their immediate supervisor as "very important" or "important" to their job satisfaction. (SHRM, 2016)

If you are still stuck on the first bullet, you should be. That statement, by itself, should justify every penny of investment you make in your supervisors.

Key Takeaway

There is a complete disconnect between the value of supervisors and the investment decisions related to their development.

Chapter 2

How We Fail Our Supervisors

"Leadership and learning are indispensable to one another."
– John F. Kennedy

Given how important supervisors are to an organization's success, why isn't selection, training, and support of those individuals a high priority in every company?

Supervisors come into their first supervisory job from one of two sources: they are selected from line workers or they move directly into supervision without working a front-line job first. This last often happens with college graduates, like me. However, most supervisors work their way up from the line. Regardless of how a person is selected for the job, the needed skills are the same.

Leadership chooses a new supervisor, sprinkles him with holy water, says, "You are now a supervisor. Go forth and conquer," and expects everything to work out. Why are we surprised when that doesn't happen? I don't believe organizations want to set their supervisors up to fail, but they do, from neglect if nothing else. We fail our supervisors in many ways.

First, our selection process is haphazard at best. The common method of choosing supervisors is to promote the person who does the front-line job the best, even though that is not the most important part of a supervisor's job. Sometimes we choose a supervisor because it's "their turn." Perhaps they are the most senior person in the work center. It may also be no one else in the work center wanted the job, so you chose the person who would say yes. These are horrible ways to choose someone for a vital leadership position.

Second, we don't lay the ground work for their success. We don't prepare them for the job, and we don't clarify our expectations. The people we promote don't know what to expect. They tend to think their new job is pretty much the same as their old job, except they can tell the other workers what to do. Just because a person is a great welder doesn't mean he can handle the paperwork, the competing priorities, or the people issues that come along with a promotion to a supervisory position.

Third, we don't give them the training they need to be successful. We may provide them with some rudimentary training, but in many organizations, we take a sink or swim approach. If we train, we focus on risk management, not the skills that can make a good supervisor a truly great supervisor. Consequently, many fail and others take way too long to learn these skills through the School of Hard Knocks.

Last, we don't provide support. You may have given them training, but translating knowledge to behavior is altogether different.

Clear performance standards (that are matched by appropriate measurement and reward) are required. Feedback, coaching and mentoring are vital.

Organizations generally do a poor job of setting expectations and providing feedback, but this is especially bad with a new supervisor because the difference between the previous job and the new one is vast.

This is compounded by the fact that we have a tendency to pull the person out of the familiar and drop them into the deep end of the pool without teaching them to dog paddle, let alone teach them a nice strong breast stroke. It is no wonder so many new supervisors drown before they learn to swim.

We'll talk about the factors that keep supervisors from succeeding in Chapter 4.

Organizations fail their new supervisors by not determining the skills required for success and using those as criteria for selection. Although technical competence is important for first-line supervisors, they don't have to be the most competent person in the work center in terms of doing the job.

Instead, we need to focus on those skills that better predict success—not just for the supervisor, but for the work center they will oversee. So, what competencies are better predictors of success? We'll talk about this more in Chapter 5.

None of these are likely to be well developed in new supervisors, but we should be able to see the promise and then develop those skills in the job.

How can we do a better job by our supervisors? In the coming chapters we'll discuss how to set up a system to do just that.

Key Takeaway

We fail supervisors by:

- Not selecting supervisors correctly
- Not preparing them for their new role
- Not setting clear expectations
- Not providing appropriate training
- Not providing adequate support

Chapter 3

Trust: The Foundation

"Whoever is careless with the truth in small matters cannot be trusted with important matters." – Albert Einstein

Before we go any further, let's talk trust.

This is the shortest chapter in the book—and the most important.

The fundamental issue that underlies most of a supervisor's success is trust. It is the foundation upon which everything else is built. This is the one attribute that must be in the character of the person you are considering for a supervisory position. It may also be one of the more difficult for those above the supervisory candidate to measure.

In a previous job, three of us were section chiefs in one unit. Two of us could not stand the third. He was likeable enough, but we didn't trust him.

We knew if he promised to take care of something, we couldn't count on it. We knew he would blow his timelines, and we would have to do our part with less time.

He would make a statement without regard to whether it was true, so we had to double check the "facts" he gave us. We didn't trust him and neither did his own people.

For the same reasons, he wasn't dependable and you couldn't be sure what he told you was entirely true. He would throw one of his people under the bus in a heartbeat. But our boss loved him because he talked a good game. He knew what to say and how to say it, so the boss believed him.

Eventually, this behavior came back to bite him, but he did a lot of damage until then through lost productivity.

In some of my training classes, I have participants list the attributes of the person they consider to be the best supervisor they ever had; then we discuss the worst supervisor. Everything the participants mention falls on one side of the question of trust or the other.

If I do not trust my supervisor, I will not take risks. I will not bring problems to his attention. I will be careful about following his instructions. I am constantly in "cover my backside" mode.

When you consider someone for the critical position of a supervisor, first determine her trustworthiness.

If she is not trustworthy, don't make the mistake of trying to turn her into a decent supervisor.

If you find you were mistaken after the promotion, it's time to cut your losses. Immediately.

Key Takeaway

If a person isn't trustworthy, he isn't supervisory material. Period.

Chapter 4

Making the Transition from Worker to Supervisor

"The hardest part of moving up the ladder is knowing what to hand off to someone else (or even to automate.) Most of us assume that as the boss, we have to do everything. The reality is that we're responsible for everything—but who actually does the work isn't important." – Thursday Bram

Although I began my work life as a supervisor, most people move into a supervisory position from a front-line worker position.

This has some advantages.

The supervisor knows the work. In fact, the new supervisor is often chosen because he is very good at the job. Unfortunately, there are also very real problems with moving from the front line to supervisor.

Most people who are promoted into their first management positions have unrealistic expectations of the job.

As a front-line worker, our perception of the supervisor's job is skewed. Many feel the supervisor's only job is to tell other people what to do, but it is much more complex.

It is often a rude awakening to find what comes along with being the boss. It shouldn't be a surprise—we should be preparing prospective supervisors for the realities of being in charge of the work center before they assume the role.

Probably one of the biggest shocks is that the boss isn't really the boss. Almost all of us have people above us, and we're caught between them and the people we supervise.

Some days it seems as if we can't make anyone happy.

There are many stressors about moving into a supervisory position for the first time. The lack of preparation means we are unprepared for the realities of the job.

I often assign the article "Becoming the Boss" by Linda Hill as a reading assignment for my leadership development program. It usually elicits some good discussions about what people expected the job of first-line supervisor to entail versus the reality they faced when promoted.

We'll discuss three of the bigger hurdles to being successful at the job.

- The supervisor's job is no longer only about the technical aspects of the job.
- It can be difficult for the new supervisor to move into an unfamiliar role when it is so easy to fall back into the familiar.
- The friend and coworker relationship with fellow workers can interfere with some of the tough calls supervisors have to make.

The Supervisor's Job is No Longer Only About the Technical Aspects of the Job

When we choose a supervisor because of her technical expertise, we are doing so often because we feel that an expert in the task will ensure the work is done correctly.

However, the supervisor's job is no longer just about getting the technical tasks done, it is about getting *others* to get them done—an entirely different skill set.

Organizations fail their new supervisors by not setting and using appropriate criteria when selecting them for the job. Although technical competence is important for first-line supervisors, they don't have to be the most competent in terms of doing the job.

Instead, we need to focus on those skills that better predict success—not just for the supervisor, but for the work center they will oversee.

So, what competencies are better predictors of success?

There are some decent models out there, but when selecting a supervisor, we need to consider their emotional intelligence, their ability to develop and maintain professional relationships, their ability to communicate, their adaptability to change, and their ability to train, coach, and develop others.

None of these skills are likely to be well-developed in new supervisors, but we should be able to see the promise and then develop those skills on the job.

We'll talk about how to do that in Chapters 5 and 6.

It's Difficult to Move into an Unfamiliar Role

The role of supervisor is distinctly different than that of a line worker. The work is not only more complex and less concrete, but there are new skills to learn and a lot of pressure managing multiple priorities.

Many new supervisors get so frustrated by the unfamiliar demands that they fall back into the comfort of the familiar. Although many small companies may need a "working supervisor," many supervisors spend more time on routine technical tasks because it is comfortable for them. It's what they know they can do well.

Consequently, they don't always spend the time on their supervisory tasks—they aren't sure what those tasks are or how to do them, leading to avoidance.

Another outcome of selecting the most technically competent person is that they have an even more difficult time allowing others to do the work (i.e., to delegate). They feel surrendering the work to others who are less skilled will lead to lower quality. This is because their focus is still on the technical task, not higher level tasks like developing others.

This is the organization's fault. We should be outlining our expectations, preparing people for the job, and coaching them to success. We don't.

Friend and Coworker Relationships Can Interfere With Tough Calls

The move from friend to boss is a hard one. As a worker, we tend to have an "us" (worker) vs. "them" (management) mentality. Suddenly, the supervisor is a "them."

Our relationships with fellow employees are important and provide a lot of satisfaction, and then they change. The dynamics of the relationship change, and often the supervisor isn't prepared for that to happen.

I am not one to say there can be no personal relationship between a supervisor and the people they supervise, but there does need to be a line. Some people can handle a fuzzy line; some need a solid demarcation.

We need to be sure we help people navigate the transition and ensure they realize they are responsible for upholding the organization's values and objectives. Sometimes this means their employees are not going to like the decisions made. Others will try to take advantage of the new supervisor, relying on their personal relationship to bend (or break) the rules.

This is one of the reasons careful consideration of a person's emotional intelligence and the ability to confront issues is important in selecting new supervisors.

How We Can Help

We can help employees transitioning from worker to supervisor by ensuring we discuss this transition with them and by providing training and coaching on how to handle the change. We need to set clear expectations.

Establishing a support system with other supervisors is a big help. Those that have been through the experience can provide a listening ear and advice.

Key Takeaway

Making the transition from worker to supervisor is hard, and made harder through lack of preparation for the role.

Chapter 5

Requisites for Success

"Knowing what you want is the first step toward getting it." – Mae West

Our first task in setting the stage for a smooth transition into a supervisory role is to choose wisely. Most of our issues with any employee can be eliminated by just choosing the right person.

Oh, to have that crystal ball! If I could choose the right person every single time, I would be a gazillionaire.

Although I may not be omniscient, I can greatly improve my odds by being clear about what I need to have in my supervisory positions.

According to *Frontline Managers: Are They Given the Leadership Tools to Succeed?*, companies fail to choose the right candidate with the right talent 82% of the time.

The authors of the report conclude that only about 10% of people have the talent to lead. Another 20% exhibit some characteristics that can be nurtured with some training and coaching.

If you choose someone from this third of the talent pool, as we noted in Chapter 1, they will contribute 48% higher profit than average managers. Wow!

As we said earlier, although our early success as a front-line worker depends upon our ability to do a job well, our success as a supervisor depends upon getting <u>others</u> to do that job well. An entirely different type of work.

So, what skills should we be looking for?

Most of our supervisors are promoted from within. When we begin looking for a new supervisor, instead of looking for the person who is the best technician, look for the person who seems to be the informal leader in your work center.

Who do other employees turn to for help with problems? Who do they go to for training? Who do they listen to when there is a change in policy and procedure? I want to carefully consider this person, because the employees have already moved her into a leadership role themselves.

The next key is to know what you're looking for, before you start looking. Too many companies don't have a clear picture of what is takes to be a successful supervisor in their organization.

Be clear about the competencies that are important in your company and how you judge a person's capability before you evaluate candidates. If you don't have this clear picture in mind, you will be more easily taken in by someone who can talk a good game.

Look for someone who shows skill in the key competencies required for success in the job. They include:

- Communication
- Collaboration
- Customer service
- Expertise/continuous learning
- Process excellence
- Staff development

Let's look at these in more detail.

Communication

Communication is key.

In order to direct work, train, handle conflict, and the myriad other supervisory duties, clear, concise communication is vital.

If I had to choose the most important communication skill, it would be listening. If you think back to the best/worst supervisor exercise in "Trust: the Foundation," people would describe the best supervisors by saying, "She really listened to me when I needed to discuss a problem."

Conversely, the worst supervisor "didn't want to hear any of my ideas or problems." Does the candidate you're considering listen well?

Although many new supervisors worry about standing in front of a group, giving a presentation, most supervisors do few presentations beyond a tool box meeting. There is nothing formal about that, and most seem comfortable speaking in that environment.

In most organizations, first line supervisors do not give many (if any) formal presentations. So this is not a skill that will rank high on the list of selection criteria in most companies (keeping in mind that every company is different).

First-line supervisors need to be able to talk to people one-on-one. It is more their ability to relate, to ask questions, and to listen that make the real difference.

It isn't necessary that a person be glib and polished in their speech. It is necessary that they can be clear about what they want.

Gaining experience in presentations may be important to developing skills for the next job, but is less critical than their ability to get their point across one-on-one or within small groups. In this case, what we need is someone who can engage their brain before opening their mouth.

Easier said than done.

I tend to avoid putting people who are easy to anger into supervisory positions—they tend to say and do things that get them and the organization into trouble.

However, this can be overcome if the person recognizes this as a fault and is willing to work at it.

The ability to write does seem to begin to trip up many people when they become supervisors. Most front-line employees have little need to write beyond filling out forms and writing some email.

Supervisors often write reports, performance appraisals, disciplinary actions, work instructions, and email. These documents matter.

It will be easier if you choose someone who can communicate clearly in writing, but if the person has other necessary skills, you can teach them to write. Just don't turn them loose without supervision in this area for a while.

New supervisors need to understand that poor spelling and grammar affects their credibility up the chain, and what they put into writing is a record they may have to answer to in any investigations, government inquiries or lawsuits.

Customer Service

By customer, I mean anyone who uses a work center's product or service. That doesn't have to mean the same person who buys your company's products and services.

Everyone on your company's team needs to be focused on that external customer, but for many work centers, their focus is on supporting the overall effort by providing support to other internal departments.

This is another area where there is a big change from front-line worker to supervisor. Many new supervisors have trouble broadening their focus from their individual job to the success of the entire enterprise.

When I start my leadership development program for new supervisors, one of the key behaviors many companies want to see by the end of the course is "being able to see the big picture."

This can be coached, but you need to start with someone who is willing to discuss changes to processes, most especially those that have an impact on their work. If they are willing to change how they do things to improve how the work center operates, then they are likely to carry that mindset into a larger role.

Expertise/Continuous Learning

One of the things front-line employees want is for their supervisor to be a resource for them—a person to go to with questions and problems.

When I went into the Air Force, the NCO that was charged with training me said I needed to learn everyone's job and be able to do their jobs as well or better than they could. I devoted myself to that, but later decided that was going a little overboard.

Yes, I do need to know what they do. I do need to know enough to be a resource. But I have since developed the belief that if I have to do everyone's job, why do I need them?

I need to know how to get the tools, equipment, and supplies they need. I need to know where to go to get answers. If I don't know something, I need to know who does.

That's what I need to know.

From an organizational point of view, I need supervisors with a broader, more systems view toward their jobs. I also need people who won't let their expertise get out of date.

I want my supervisors to be reading, talking to others, and learning new technology and processes. I want them to learn from others and pass on that learning. I want them to be good teachers.

I need them to value and reward good ideas, even those they didn't come up with and perhaps don't agree with.

Process Excellence

I said I didn't want or expect the supervisor to be the best technician, but then I say process excellence is a core competency.

Although this may sound like I am contradicting myself, I'm not. I am not talking about a supervisor able to do the job herself, but having a focus on high-quality, timely, and efficient work.

In addition, I want her to be looking for new, better ways of doing the work all of the time. Whether they themselves come up with creative, innovative ideas, or improve and pass on the ideas of the people who work for them, I never want to hear, "If it isn't broke, why fix it?"

Staff Development

The primary role of every supervisor is to grow and develop the people who work for them.

I often ask the supervisors I coach, "Who could take your place if you don't make it to work tomorrow?"

The answer is often, "No one."

Sometimes supervisors want this to be true because they don't feel secure in their jobs. As one supervisor told me, "I'm not going to tell people everything I know. When the next layoff happens, I'm going to be the last man standing because they can't get by without me and they know it. If I train other people to do the things I do, then I could be the one looking for a job."

In some cases, they may say their lead could keep the production process moving for a while, but the other supervisory tasks would not get done.

When I hear "no one," my response is, "Then you're not doing your job."

It does happen that you may have a small work center in which no one currently there wants the supervisor's job. That's okay. I don't want to promote someone into a position they do not want, but if that is the case, I need to look elsewhere in my company for talent that may be able to make a move or I need to be prepared to go outside the company for a replacement when the time comes.

I do not want to force someone into the job who isn't interested.

One of the statements that makes me insane is, "I don't have time to train."

We have time to fire and rehire. We have time to redo work. We have time to deal with customer complaints.

But we don't have time to train? That's idiotic.

One key aspect of training is cross training. Not only should each person know their job, there should be at least one other person who can do the job (even if not as well) for every position.

There is no excuse for a customer to need assistance or to have an order that needs to go out and the process is at a standstill because someone is on vacation. None.

Bottom line? Choose your new supervisors with care. Choose someone competent in some aspect of the job, but put more emphasis on choosing someone who has the attributes to be a good supervisor, regardless of their technical skills.

Key Takeaway

Although we can never be absolutely certain that a person will be a great supervisor, we can improve our chances by looking for the informal leader and focusing on supervisor competencies instead of technical skills and/or seniority.

Chapter 6

Supervisor Training and Development

"As there is no insignificant work, there is not an insignificant leader. All leaders need training...not just a few." - Quint Studer

When I was responsible for supervisor training in a previous place of employment, I put new supervisors through an initial training, primarily focused on compliance.

Each month, we had a supervisor's meeting, which included some training and also discussion on some issue where supervisors could share their ideas and experiences.

Looking back at that, it wasn't nearly enough, although it was more than most organizations have.

Once you anoint someone as a supervisor, you are responsible for the things he says and does in the performance of his job. This is a key reason companies should be careful when selecting their supervisors.

Every supervisor should receive training before they become a supervisor, and on a regular basis thereafter. Training and development should be targeted to the needs of the supervisor. To the training community, there is a difference between training and development.

Training is focused on knowledge. Development is focused on skill development. For the purposes of this book, I am going to use the terms interchangeably.

Training should be focused both on reducing risk and improving performance.

The areas supervisors need training in can be summarized with the 6 C's of Training: Compliance, Communication, Collaboration, Conflict, Change and Coaching.

I used to have 5 C's, but over time have found of the concept of Collaboration important enough to separate it out for emphasis.

You'll note that with the exception of Compliance, all of these areas are skills that fall under the umbrella of leadership. We are really training supervisors on leadership and adding knowledge about compliance.

But wait, haven't there been a lot of articles lately that say leadership training doesn't work? Well, yes, there have.

As a general statement about the way most organizations do leadership training, I agree; leadership training doesn't work. But that doesn't mean it <u>can't</u> work.

Here are the reasons I see that the expenditure many companies make in leadership training doesn't yield the results they expect.

First, they invest in leadership <u>training.</u>

Training helps people acquire knowledge. It doesn't mean the participant has the ability to apply that knowledge, or that the organization will allow it.

I can pass on great information, you can take notes and memorize all of it, but if you cannot apply it in the workplace, it's useless.

I am not saying training has no value. Knowledge forms a solid foundation on which to build.

Training has to be supplemented with developmental activities, coaching, and support. In other words, the participant has to have the opportunity to use what they learned, and someone needs to provide some coaching in order for them to become proficient.

The next thing that keeps leadership training from being effective is that most of it is applied at the wrong level of the organization.

Most leadership training is attended by senior managers. Yes, they need to know how to be better leaders. Yes, they have influence.

The assumption is that if we teach the people at the top how to lead better, that knowledge will trickle down to the rest of the organization.

It doesn't.

The people with the most influence in an organization and who touch the most people are the first-line supervisors.

They need the training (and accompanying development) most. That is the level at which better leadership skills will have the most impact. But we don't do much leadership training and development at that level.

We use the School of Hard Knocks approach and keep trading out supervisors until one of them "gets it" quickly enough to perform satisfactorily before they get fired.

Last, almost all leadership training focuses on one person--the leader. I did a search for pictures of leaders, and most of the ones that came up had a picture of one person—a person who looks like a leader, I assume.

In pictures where there was more than one person, the leader is at the front—large, in focus, and serious. One can assume the fuzzy little people behind her are her "followers." That's the fundamental problem with leadership training. It focuses too much on the leader.

Leadership is a group activity. We don't spend enough time talking about how leadership functions in a group. Leadership is the art of influencing people to willingly work toward a common goal. And people are not one-size-fits-all.

People in a group (or team) are different than when they are alone. That's why it is so important that those learning about leadership actually lead.

The information they get in training gives them new tools to try. Practice allows them to become proficient. If they have a skilled coach, they'll become proficient faster, with less frustration.

Back to our original issue. No, leadership training by itself doesn't show much return on investment.

In order for it to pay off, you have to also invest in development, and you have to spread the leadership training around the organization, especially to those with the greatest touch in the organization—first-line supervisors.

Now, let's look in more detail at what should be included in each of the 6 C's.

Compliance

Compliance is probably where companies do best in training their supervisors. The types of training included in this area are those mandated by law or regulation, as well as training relating to reducing the risk associated with the supervisor's role.

Compliance is fairly mechanical. You *are* or you *are not* in compliance with laws, regulations, and policies. Compliance is purely an effort to control risk. We hope that by providing this training, supervisors will not do things that garner complaints to regulatory agencies or land us in court.

Compliance training is not a "one and done" item. Many compliance items don't come up often, so supervisors need regular reminders of specific areas of concern. Laws, regulations, and policies also change—regular, updated training needs to be done to be sure supervisors are current in their knowledge.

I am not a fan of more is better when it comes to compliance training. We often err in training by giving the supervisor more information than they need. They are not the HR professional, nor the company lawyer.

They need information that applies to them and the types of situations they will encounter in their day-to-day work. And then, they need to know who to call if they encounter a situation outside the norm.

If your company doesn't have an HR professional on staff to help your supervisors, you will need to provide more training or hire some outside expertise.

At the very minimum, supervisors should have some training in:

- **Ethics**. I start with this one. I know many companies do not make a concerted effort in this area, but as employees tend to follow the ethical practices they see, not the practices written in your code of conduct, ensuring your supervisors thoroughly understand your company code of conduct and their role in modeling the appropriate behaviors is critical. The supervisor is the person your employees see every day. The supervisor is the person who has to know an ethical issue when she sees it and know what to do. Do not skimp on this.

- **Equal Employment Opportunity/Sexual Harassment**. Most companies make this entirely too long. Supervisors need to know what the policy says, what type of behavior is not acceptable and what to do/not do if someone comes to them with a complaint. They need to understand what retaliation is. It doesn't take hours to do this. In fact, I find that the longer the training is, the less they remember. I can do this training in 20 minutes. It covers what they need to know, without a bunch of fluff to obscure the message.

- **Fair Labor Standards Act (FLSA).** This is the single largest area of employment law liability for a company. Supervisors need to understand your company's policies on pay (I am assuming your policies comply with the statute). Again, focus on the items that most closely affect them. For example, "Yes, we must pay people for all time worked, regardless of where or when that work takes place." Therefore, supervisors absolutely cannot request nor allow people to work off the clock.

- **Other Employment Laws that Apply to Your Company**. Whoever handles your HR should sit down and make a list of the laws of concern and what the supervisor needs to know. For example, don't train them on Family Medical Leave if you are not a covered employer. But if you are a covered employer, what does the supervisor need to know? They need to have a good idea when FMLA may apply and when people are eligible—but they should have just enough knowledge to know when to refer the employee to the person who administers the program for a detailed analysis and to get information about the administrative requirements. Supervisors need to know how to account for the time in the payroll system. And they need to understand what constitutes retaliation and that it is not permitted. That's it.

- **Company Policies**. Don't assume supervisors have read, let alone understand, your employee handbook. Regular refresher training on policies needs to be built into your training schedule. Obviously, when policies change, supervisors need to know. Your supervisors are the ones who will be getting the complaints and the questions about policies, so they need to have accurate information about the policy and why it is important. If you can't explain why the policy is important, ditch the policy, because your supervisors are going to have a hard time explaining it and your employees are likely to resent it.

- **Discipline and Termination**. This is part of company policies, but I separate them out because there is more involved than just knowing company policies about discipline. There is a certain level of skill here. The goal of discipline is to change behavior, so it is not just a matter of knowing the administrative details of applying discipline, but learning how to discuss discipline with the employee to be sure the employee can take the correction to heart. By the time we get to termination, we aren't looking to change behavior, but how we go about terminating employees can make a big difference in possible complaints or lawsuits later, our company's reputation with our workforce and in the community, as well as the likelihood of violent behavior.

Communication

It should come as no surprise that one of the areas on which I spend a lot of time in my supervisor coaching practice is communication. It isn't always what a supervisor says that causes a problem, but the way she says it.

Communication is such an all-encompassing topic, it can be intimidating. Although there are many areas in communication, there are certain key areas that are vitally important to first-line supervisors.

As I stated earlier, most first-line supervisors don't have to be polished presenters—most of their verbal communication is one-on-one or in more informal, small group meetings. However, for many supervisors, a new and intimidating type of communication is writing.

There are many jobs in which the ability to write clearly and concisely is not very important, but as a supervisor, writing reports, disciplinary actions, emails, and performance appraisals can be fraught with problems.

Some of the issues in communication that are common with new supervisors are due to how we think more than our abilities in communicating.

Here are two examples.

- **The "everybody knows" syndrome.** By the time many people become supervisors, they have been in the workforce for some time. They have gained experience about the expectations of the workplace in general and about the expectations of their workplace specifically. A fundamental barrier to communication is the "everybody knows" syndrome. We assume that because we know, everyone else should know. I don't need to tell my employees they need to be on time, because "everybody knows" you have to be on time for work. I don't have to tell someone that their dress is not appropriate because "everybody knows" what the correct dress is in our workplace. Many of us cannot remember that we didn't know either until someone told us. This is often one of the barriers to being clear about expectations and priorities. We assume the people who work for us have the same knowledge and experience.

- **"I shouldn't have to tell someone more than once" syndrome**. Yes, you do need to tell someone more than once. If you study marketing, you'll hear the adage that a consumer has to be exposed to a message at least seven times before it sticks—preferably more. Just like us, employees have a lot of messages bombarding them and their brains filter out the majority of them, especially if they don't particularly like the message. In addition, not everyone is an auditory learner. Instructions that are only heard don't always stick. Repetition is necessary.

If there is one skill supervisors need to work on, it is listening. Most of us think we are good listeners. We are not. When I ask employees if their supervisor is a good listener, most say no. Why is that?

Many times it is because supervisors are trying to do multiple things at once. Supervisors think they can multi-task.

Study after study has shown this not to be the case, but even if we can, we shouldn't. When we do something else while an employee is talking to us, the employee perceives we are not listening.

Employees equate listening with our perception of their value. If we listen, we value them.

If it appears we are not listening, we do not value them. So they stop talking to us.

Collaboration

Frequently, at the front-line worker level, one can get away with being a lone wolf. That doesn't work well once a person moves into a supervisory role.

Collaboration is vital. Not only do supervisors need to work well with their own people, they need to work well with others throughout the organization, which requires a broader view of the organization and our role within it.

I originally lumped collaboration-related skills into the other areas, but over time, I have come to the realization this is an important skill that needs to be emphasized.

Collaboration includes things like:

- Being able to see the big picture
- Building and maintaining relationships
- Teamwork

Just because we can communicate well with individuals doesn't mean we can build a network of interlocking people in order to get things done.

Earlier, I talked about the importance of being able to see the bigger picture of how all of the departments need to work together to get things done for our customers.

Companies do not spend money on departments and people they do not think are necessary, so whether we can see their value or not, those with the ability to decide on the allocation of resources apparently do, so we need to figure it out.

Many supervisors don't work well with people they do not like, whether that person works for them or is a manager in another department. It is vital that a supervisor learns that liking isn't necessary—collaboration is.

Even with people we know and like, effort to build and maintain good relationships greases the wheels of cooperation in the workplace.

Supervisors should have a grasp of Networking 101 principles and how those principles translate into making their job easier.

Although companies have put a lot of emphasis on the concept of teamwork, they do not do a good job of teaching people to work in teams. A group of people working in the same area does not constitute a team.

The issue here is that Americans are taught to work alone. All through school, we hear, "Do your own work." We are graded on what we did—collaboration is cheating.

But somehow, once we are in the workplace, we are expected to know how to work as a part of a team. In order to effectively model and teach teamwork skills, we need to teach our supervisors about teams and how to lead them to high performance. A tall order.

A key part of building relationships and working as a team is an appreciation for diversity. I don't use that term only in the sense of race or gender, which is the way most people view the term.

I use the term diversity to mean, "everyone's different." And because of that, we have the opportunity to be creative and innovative.

Conflict

One of the greatest areas of supervisor fears is handling conflict. Most supervisors are conflict-averse.

This is another area where mindset is the fundamental problem. Many people assume if there is conflict, it is a bad thing. Conflict can indeed be a drain on productivity and lead to all sorts of problems, most of which fall upon the supervisor to deal with.

However, conflict is also the basis for problem solving and creativity.

If there was no conflict, there would be no change and no improvement. My husband and I have been married for 37 years. He is the love of my life, but that certainly doesn't mean we always see eye to eye. It does mean we have to have ways to ensure the conflict doesn't harm our relationship.

It's the same thing in the workplace. If you have two people, there will be conflict. It is normal. The supervisor's job is to manage the conflict so that it remains a positive element instead of escalating into World War III.

Most supervisors do not have the skills to handle conflict in a positive way. Appropriate training and coaching are vital.

Change

We talked in the last chapter about process excellence being a core competency for supervisors. That means we are always looking for a better way. A better way is a different way, which means change.

Supervisors are vital to any change effort, but most are not prepared for the ways they can help their employees accept and implement change in the workplace.

Most managers seem to believe that just announcing a change is enough to make it happen. Not so. It is no wonder most organizational change efforts fail.

It is easy enough to buy new facilities or equipment. It is not hard to redesign processes. The difficult piece is the people who have to operate the equipment or use the new process.

We need to train supervisors on the realities of how change works, why people resist change, how to garner support for change, and how to embed the new process in the way we work.

If change doesn't happen at the work center level, it doesn't happen in the organization either.

Supervisors are in a key position to communicate the change and to enlist support. Often when rolling out a change, we do not sell the first-line supervisors. We just announce the change. We put them in a position to have to tell their people, "Just do it."

Enlisting the aid of your supervisors, and subsequently the people who work for them, is a necessary part of making change work.

Coaching

We want supervisors to develop the people who work for them, but we don't help them learn and develop the crucial art of coaching.

Coaching is improving performance. Coaching requires the coach to focus on each person's strengths.

We tend to focus on our employees' shortcomings. If you have a supervisor who sees only what people do wrong, they will not excel at developing high performance in their work center.

There are a number of skills required to do a good job of coaching: goal setting, feedback, questioning, delegation, etc.

The best way for supervisors to learn to coach is to have the behavior modeled by those above them, but as we have said before, that often doesn't happen.

Trust is a vital component of coaching—on both sides of the coaching relationship.

Don't Overlook the Value of Experiential Learning

We tend to think about training as a classroom exercise, or in some cases, an online course. Certainly, that is an important component.

Structured training courses can help provide some standardization to training and help ensure everyone gets the benefit of the same information. However, classroom learning by itself is easily forgotten and often not implemented.

Adults learn by observing and by doing.

As an example, if you want your supervisors to learn to see the big picture and to lead teams, put them on cross-functional teams *led by someone who understands how teams work and can model the necessary behaviors.*

This is sometimes our difficulty—we don't have managers with these skills to start with. Exposing supervisors to bad examples can show them what <u>not</u> to do, but that doesn't necessarily mean they will come out of the experience having any idea of what they <u>should</u> do.

When we give supervisors an experiential activity, we need to be clear it is not just more work. We need to set clear expectations of what they can contribute and what we want them to learn.

Having regular coaching sessions to discuss your supervisor's experiences and what he has learned can help emphasize the importance of the experience and show the applicability of what is being learned.

The School of Hard Knocks works, but it can be painful. Experiential activities permit much of this learning to be done in a more controlled environment, making it safer for the supervisor and the company.

Helping Supervisors Apply Learning

The hardest part of learning is applying what we are taught to the workplace. Companies often send people to classes, but don't see a change when people come back to work.

I often have supervisors in my development courses balk at doing some of the techniques we talk about in class in their work centers. It is difficult, because in many cases, we are asking them to break old habits and take a risk to try something new, often in an environment that doesn't support the change.

This is where regular feedback and coaching come in. Expectations to put these skills into play need to be set. Regular feedback and coaching will show how to apply the techniques in specific situations and reinforce the behaviors we want.

We'll talk about this in more detail in the next chapter.

Leadership Development Ladder

Do you have a systematic process for growing the leaders at all levels of the organization? If not, you should.

The table on the next two pages is an outline.

You don't have to follow it precisely, as every organization is different, but this gives you a way to approach training.

In this plan, I have emphasized preparation and the first-line supervisor, although I did add at least the beginnings of a broad approach for levels above the first-line supervisor.

Leadership Development Plan		
Career Level	Focus	Suggested Activities
Everyone	Laying the foundation— everyone is a leader.	Classes/coaching on teams, conflict, and communication. Participation in problem-solving discussions and teams.
Preparatory (not yet a supervisor)	Developing knowledge and skills important to first-line supervisors. Develop knowledge about what the supervisor role entails.	Classes on teams, conflict, communication, and process improvement. Assign as a lead (or second in command). Delegation of some first-line tasks, such as scheduling, training, etc. Short periods filling in during the supervisor's absence, with appropriate oversight. Assignment to cross-functional teams involving the work center.
New first-line supervisor	Ensuring the supervisor has the knowledge and skills to be successful in a completely new role.	Classes on compliance, coaching, goal-setting, as well as continued training as stated for previous levels.

Experienced first-line supervisor	Talent management and staff development. Build and maintain broad relationships. Develop better understanding of the organization and its stakeholders.	Continue all previous. Consider assigning as a mentor to new supervisors. Assign to cross-functional teams at higher levels or across broader aspects of the organization. Delegate tasks from the next higher level to determine aptitude, broader vision, and to develop broader relationships across the organization.
Preparation for higher leadership position	Develop understanding of the company, its stakeholders and the industry. Begin developing higher level strategy and communication skills.	Continue leadership training. Assign to cross-functional teams on organizational issues. Consider assigning to leadership development opportunities outside the organization, such as nonprofit boards or community projects. A good time to begin improving presentation skills (Possible resource: Toastmasters International)

Mutual Aid and Support

I cannot emphasize how important it is that supervisors have a support structure in place to help them succeed. We'll talk about that more in the next chapter. One good way to do that is a regular supervisor meeting, with a little bit of training mixed with a good amount of discussion.

Summary

In order to have a successful supervisor training program, companies need to clearly identify the knowledge, skills, and competencies needed by supervisors in their company. I summarized the most important ones in this chapter, but every company has its own culture that needs to be considered in developing their training program.

Training is not a "one and done" affair. Companies need to take a life cycle approach to training, with periodic refresher training in the area of compliance, and regular coaching and reinforcement in the skills noted earlier in this chapter.

If your company promotes from within, you have an opportunity to identify people with the potential to be good supervisors early, and to prepare them for a supervisory position before they are thrust into the role.

Once they are promoted, a training plan with courses in all of the above areas is essential, supplemented with regular feedback and coaching. Regular refresher training, discussion, and problem solving through monthly or quarterly meetings are helpful. In the next chapter, we'll discuss how to keep our supervisors focused on fulfilling their responsibilities and improving their skills.

Key Takeaway

Most supervisor training is too narrowly focused on compliance. Training should encompass all Six C's: Compliance, Communication, Collaboration, Conflict, Change and Coaching.

Chapter 7

Supervisor Support

"Because a thing seems difficult for you, do not think it impossible for anyone to accomplish." – Marcus Aurelius

Even those companies that do a fair job of selecting and training their supervisors sometimes let them down through inadequate support. I don't believe any company purposely sets out to undermine their supervisors or to make their jobs harder, but it happens.

As we discussed in Chapter 1, although senior organizational leadership understands intellectually that there is a huge gap between the knowledge and skills first-line supervisors need and their abilities, they act illogically by failing to provide the resources necessary to help supervisors be successful.

Leadership support is critical to ensuring we have supervisors who can provide the leadership necessary to motivate their work teams to work at a high level of performance on a regular basis.

How can we do a better job of supporting our supervisors? There are some specific areas every organization should consider and in which they should make deliberate decisions about the systems they put into place. The specific areas companies need to consider are:

- Selection
- Training and Development
- Coaching
- Accountability
- Rewards and Recognition

We discussed the first two items in this list earlier in the book. In this chapter, we'll tackle the last three.

Coaching

Coaching is all about improving performance by focusing on the specific skills needed to achieve success. Generally, there is someone who acts as a coach to help the person being coached evaluate their current performance, determine their strengths, set goals, and provide feedback. In order to be successful, coaching requires a few things. First is a trusting relationship between the coach and the person being coached.

Obviously, we want the supervisor to be able to coach their people. We talked about that in Chapter 5. In this chapter, we're concerned with coaching the supervisor. Supervisors do not step into their role perfect. None of us do—that's an unrealistic expectation.

Coaching can only be successful when certain conditions are met. First, the person being coached has to have good self-awareness, or at least be open to feedback about how others perceive them.

They also need to be willing to accept responsibility for making a change. If a person cannot or will not see their behavior through the eyes of others or believes their shortcomings are "not my fault," then coaching is doomed to failure. You have what you have.

Any improvement will come at the expense of a lot of time and effort, and will probably have only mediocre impact.

Who should provide the coaching? Ideally, the supervisor's manager. If the trust factor is there and the manager has the skills, then they should be the primary coach. If you are selecting supervisors for their ability to coach, one might assume those higher in the hierarchy would also be selected in part on their ability to coach performance in their direct reports.

There is a certain reluctance with most of us to admit faults to our boss. We may not feel safe to do so. We may not be completely honest, because part of our performance issues may be because of our boss.

A safer alternative may be someone outside the chain of command. I would not want that person to be the primary coach, but certainly, they can provide additional perspective and help.

If you are a large enough organization, coaching should be a primary responsibility of your HR manager. They should have the skills to conduct this type of coaching and the reputation for confidentiality to allow a supervisor to admit to insecurity and errors.

Again, if you don't have this resource inside your company, consider outside help.

Your coach can help the supervisor by role-playing difficult conversations. How should Jane approach John about his lack of personal hygiene? What about discussing how to have a disciplinary conversation with Susie, who tends to become defensive?

The ability to provide a safe place to practice a conversation and to discuss options is important. If a supervisor has a script in their mind before engaging in tough conversations, they are more likely to be successful in achieving the desired result.

As we mentioned in Chapter 6, feedback is an important component in coaching. Regular feedback is just as important for supervisors as it is for any other employee.

Supervisors need timely, constructive feedback as much as anyone, but often don't get it for many of the same reasons we don't give feedback—it takes time we don't think we have, we don't think we should need to, we worry about hurting feelings, or we are concerned about the push back.

Feedback also needs to be done correctly to be effective.

Setting Expectations

Are the supervisor's responsibilities to grow and develop their people clearly spelled out? Just like supervisors assume "everybody knows" expected workplace standards, we tend to do the same with our supervisors. We assume they know what we expect. Be clear. Explain how they get the A, and then follow through with accountability.

Accountability

What gets measured, gets done. Supervisors have many competing priorities. There are usually too few hours in the day to get everything done. How do supervisors prioritize? They do it like the rest of us. They deal with the urgent issues that are in position to do them damage. In most companies, that means the focus is on results in the short term. How fast, how good, or how cheap?

We may say we want the supervisor to grow and develop their people. We may say we want them to focus on culture, communication, and employee engagement. But those are long-term goals. What do supervisors have to answer for at meetings? What Key Performance Indicators (KPIs) do their bosses pay attention to? What areas are on their evaluation forms? Odds are, they all revolve around short-term, urgent needs, and little, if any, long-term assignments.

Even if long-term items are included, the likelihood is that upper level managers will forgive not meeting those as long as the urgent numbers look good. Without attention, supervisors will default to taking care of the urgent matters over those things where the reward (or punishment) is farther out.

Look at your supervisor performance appraisals. In many companies, their appraisal looks the same as the one used for first-line employees.

The most common change made to an appraisal at the supervisory level is one rated area titled, "Supervision." As long as the supervisor doesn't do anything to get the company in trouble and they are making their production numbers, the likelihood is they will get a decent rating in this area even if their performance is lackluster..

Rewards and Recognition

This is very similar to accountability. Accountability tends to be both positive and negative. Rewards and recognition are positive—raises, promotions, praise. You might say you want certain behaviors, but what are the consequences of not developing your people? Who gets the accolades? Who gets the bonuses? Who gets promoted?

If you are like most companies, production numbers are the only thing that matters. But in truth, paying attention to those important but not urgent tasks like developing people will pay great dividends in better results in the long term.

Key Takeaway

If you don't put a support structure in place that measures and rewards critical supervisory behaviors, you will be lucky to get them. What gets measured, gets done.

Chapter 8

Let's Talk Evaluation

"No plan of operations extends with certainty beyond the first encounter with the enemy's main strength." – Helmuth von Moltke the Elder

  Throughout this book, I have talked about a systematic approach to selecting, training, and supporting supervisors. I hope it motivates you to invest in such a program. But there is an old military saying (derived from the above): "No good plan survives engagement with the enemy." Loosely translated for the purposes of this book—stuff happens.
  Not all organizations are the same. The same programs don't work equally well in all cases. Things change. Therefore, it's important to regularly review and evaluate any program. The question is how.

Possible Evaluation Metrics

  It is hard to evaluate without a baseline. Here are a few suggested measures to use as a yardstick for your new and improved supervisor success process.

Supervisor Success Ratio

A broad measurement might be, how many supervisors are considered fully successful after 18 months? That implies you have a good, solid description of what constitutes "fully successful." I chose 18 months as a baseline just because that seems to be the time when organizations decide they have made a poor hiring decision and try again.

If you believe you have a good system in place to bring your supervisors along faster, then you may choose to measure at a different time (say, at 12 months).

Employee Satisfaction/Employee Engagement Scores

If your company takes regular measurements of employee satisfaction or engagement, and you have enough employees that you can slice and dice the data to work center level without losing anonymity, then a positive change in score can indicate your efforts are gaining traction.

You would need to measure across all work centers and not just one to have a good indicator of system-wide success.

Turnover

Turnover is the number of people who leave in a given timeframe as compared to the total number of employees, expressed as a percentage.

I have some issues with turnover, because many people use it as a yardstick without fully understanding the measure. In most companies, it is given too much weight without much analysis. But it can be a measure that can be used in conjunction with other measures to give you some indicator of your program's effectiveness.

In order to be able to gauge what turnover means, you need some context. What is normal for your industry? What is the voluntary turnover versus the involuntary turnover (each can tell you something)? How is turnover among new hires versus those with longer tenure compared to the average? What about critical skills? And, of course, work center to work center.

Turnover can give you an indicator to evaluate your program, but not by itself.

Customer Satisfaction Measures

The customer is king (or queen) when it comes to marketplace competition. If you can create a tie between what customers are bragging about—or complaining about—in your organization and the contribution to this in the work center's output, then you can make some evaluation of the effectiveness of your supervisors.

Most customer satisfaction information doesn't provide sufficient detail. However, if I know what is important to my customers, I should be able to make a tie back to how that happens.

For example, if I know that on-time delivery is a critical item for my customers, then I need to track on-time delivery. Although we tend to tie that directly to operations, it isn't always operations that is the issue.

Late delivery could be due to a number of breakdowns in the system, to include purchasing, scheduling, operations, sales, or shipping. I need to know not only how many shipments were late, but the cause.

Evaluating the cause of the change over time could help indicate the success of my supervisors.

Quality Measures

All of us have measures that indicate quality. Manufacturing tends to have an entire system set up for this, but any company can determine what constitutes quality and set up measures.

The key is to be able to collect and analyze data in such a way as to determine the impact of the various work centers on the outcome. This can be more difficult than it might appear, especially in larger organizations, where multiple work centers touch a product or service.

Profitability

I use profitability instead of productivity. Productivity is how much output you get from each input. This doesn't necessarily mean you make money on the process.

Productivity tends to focus on cost cutting instead of revenue enhancement. Both are necessary, but given a choice, I will go with revenue enhancement every time. This can be a tough measure for some departments due to the way we develop financial statements, but where you can make such a measure work, it can be very insightful.

Readiness for Increased Responsibility

This is really a measurement at two levels. If you pride yourself on internal advancement, how well do you do at preparing your supervisors to move into increasing levels of responsibility?

If this is important to you, then this should be part of your evaluation—how ready are your supervisors to move into higher levels? Again, I would choose a timeframe to use as the yardstick. I would also choose some standard other than 100%. Some excel where they are and have no interest in moving up. If that's the case, fine.

By the same token, if we are going to hold supervisors accountable for talent development, then one of the criterion should be whether they are preparing people to move into their job (or another supervisory position).

Another measure may involve how well the group is cross-trained to cover one another. Are there any gaps in capability when someone is out?

You can see that deciding on the appropriate measures and deciding how to measure can be tricky, but it is an important part of evaluating your success. Because none of these changes can be made overnight, you may decide to review quarterly, or in some cases, annually.

Return on Investment

Providing you know what objectives you had for your supervisory development program and had appropriate measures in place, you should be able to calculate a return on investment.

A Checklist

Maybe it's my military mind, but I love checklists. Checklists help me sort out what's important. They help me focus on key elements I need to ensure get done. They ensure I don't overlook something important. So here is my checklist for a good supervisor program.

Like any checklist, it only helps if you use it, and you're honest. You can pencil whip this if you want, but if you want an organization that can compete on a world class level, I advise against it. Be brutally honest and then create an action plan to fix your shortcomings.

Element	Yes	No	No Idea
My organization has a systematic process to identify, prepare, select, train, and support first-line supervisors.			
Senior leadership in my organization is active in and supportive of supervisor development.			
My organization has specific objectives for our supervisor program.			
My organization has determined the needed knowledge, skills, and competencies for first-line supervisors to be successful.			
My organization devotes sufficient resources to supervisor development.			
We have written job descriptions that emphasize specific leadership responsibilities for our supervisors.			
We provide leadership development training and development to all employees—everyone is considered a leader.			
My organization has a process to identify individuals who are informal leaders in our organization.			
My organization provides developmental training to potential supervisors before they are selected for that role.			
New supervisors know exactly what is expected of them in their new role.			

New supervisors are quickly brought up to speed on compliance topics.			
Supervisors at all levels understand how their performance will be graded.			
Training and development of supervisors is structured with both knowledge and experiential aspects, and covers all 6 C's.			
Our leadership training emphasizes leadership as a group activity, not a solo enterprise.			
Our leadership training covers all levels of leadership development with appropriate courses and experiences.			
Our organization has carefully considered our reward and recognition program and how it impacts the success of our supervisors and their work teams.			
Our performance management system puts a priority on all aspects of a supervisor's performance—not just production.			
The ability to train and develop people is rewarded through our total rewards policies and practices.			
Our supervisor development program has appropriate measures to determine its success.			
We regularly evaluate our supervisor development program and make appropriate improvements.			

Key Takeaway

Every organization needs to regularly review and evaluate their supervisor development program. Constant evaluation and improvement is just as critical in your supervisor development process as it is for any other process or program.

Summary

If you had to spend a significant amount of money to achieve a 48% increase in profitability, would you do it? Would you devote a couple of hours a week to making it happen? Of course, you would!

In spite of the fact that we know supervisors are key to employee engagement, making change work, reducing turnover, and improving productivity, we invest little or nothing in ensuring we have and support the best supervisors possible. It doesn't make sense.

I challenge you to invest in putting people first, especially those who provide leadership in the trenches where the war for customers is won and lost—your first-line supervisors.

Want to Know More?

Finding resources designed for first-line supervisors can be tough. It is difficult to let supervisors go for extended periods for training. Here are two additional resources that may be helpful in your supervisory development program.

Leadership in the Trenches: Developing Front-Line Leaders (Coming Soon! Expected publication date: September 2018) Written for the first-line supervisor, this book covers a lot of must-know knowledge. Designed as a workbook, it lays the foundation with information every supervisor needs, with case studies and suggested exercises to make the supervisor more comfortable applying the information at their workplace. An excellent tool to use in conjunction with your regular supervisor trainings.

The Supervisor Academy. Developed by the author, The Supervisor Academy is a series of short, online tutorials on a variety of supervisory subjects. Works well alone, in conjunction with Leadership in the Trenches: Developing Your First-line Leadership Ability, and/or as part of your on-going supervisor training. For more information, email **admin@venturehro.com**.

Contact me! I'm happy to talk to you about your organizational needs. You can contact me at Penny@myhrdepartmentwf.com

Resources

Beck, Randall and James Harter. "Why Great Managers Are So Rare." Harvard Business Review Blog, March 13, 2014. Retrieved from http://hbr.org/2014/03/why-good-managers-are-so-rare

"Employee Job Satisfaction and Engagement: Revitalizing a Changing Workforce." Society for Human Resource Management, 2016. Retrieved from shrm.org/hr-today/trends-and-forecasting/research-and-surveys/Documents/2016-Employee-Job-Satisfaction-and-Engagement-Report.pdf

"Frontline Managers: Are They Given the Leadership Tools to Succeed?" HBR Analytic Services. Retrieved from http://hbr.org/resources/pdfs/tools/Halogen-Report-June2014.pdf

Hill, Linda. "Becoming the Boss," Harvard Business Review, January 2007.

"Manager/Supervisor's Role in Change Management." Whitepaper. Retrieved from http://prosci.com/change-managemenet/thought-leadership-library/manager-change-management-role

About the Author

   Penny Miller spent 21 years in the United States Air Force, working in the human resources arena. Her last assignment was as a squadron commander, overseeing human resources for a large installation. It was in the armed forces that she developed a deep appreciation for the first-line supervisory role and its importance in organizational excellence. That passion stayed with her in corporate HR.

   In 2007, she founded Venture HRO, later renamed My HR Department, an HR consulting company. Most of her practice centers around training and coaching organizational leaders, with her primary focus on those leading "in the trenches," where the War for Profit is waged.